Deadwood, South Dakota:

A Frontier Community

by Nomi J. Waldman

Table of Contents

Introduction

There was always something special about Deadwood. Maybe it was the way it became a town. One day there was just a **gulch**, or deep valley, in what is now western South Dakota. It was called Deadwood Gulch. Then, suddenly, there was a town in the gulch, or at least the beginnings of a town.

Maybe what made Deadwood so special was the people who settled there. They arrived from all over the world. Why? Because around 1875, they heard that gold had been found in Deadwood Gulch.

◀ Deadwood Gulch had steep sides. The gulch got its name from the dead trees on the hills.

The news that gold had been found started a **gold rush**. By 1876, people were rushing to the gulch. They were hoping to get rich. They turned Deadwood into a **frontier** (frun-TEER) community. A frontier is a place where people have just begun to settle.

Back then, Deadwood was in the Dakota **Territory** (TAIR-ih-tor-ee). A territory is a part of the country that isn't ready to be a state. It has to grow and change. It has to have laws and a government. Read on to find out what happened to this frontier community.

A Mining Community

In the 1870s, many people headed for the Dakota Territory. The government gave away land to anyone who would **homestead**, or farm, it. The gold rush brought even more people. For all those people, the frontier meant a chance to start a new life.

Most of the people who first moved to Deadwood were miners. As soon as they got there, the miners started to look for gold.

▲ As more people moved to Deadwood, log cabins started to replace tents. Deadwood was becoming a town.

Deadwood wasn't really a town yet. It was just a mining camp. Rows of tents were set up at the bottom of the gulch. The rows of tents formed Deadwood's Main Street.

The **population** (pah-pyuh-LAY-shun) kept growing. Population is a number that tells how many people live in a place. In Deadwood, the population was soon in the thousands. Deadwood became so crowded that people even set up tents on the steep sides of the gulch.

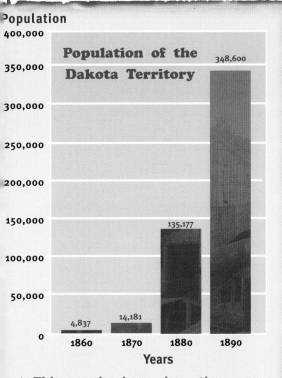

Population

Population of the Dakota Territory

- 400,000
- 350,000
- 300,000
- 250,000
- 200,000
- 150,000
- 100,000
- 50,000
- 0

Years	Population
1860	4,837
1870	14,181
1880	135,177
1890	348,600

▲ This graph shows how the population in the Dakota Territory grew after gold was discovered.

They Made a Difference

Her full name was Sarah Campbell, but she was called Aunt Sally. She was a black woman, the first non-Native American woman to come to the Black Hills, the low mountains where Deadwood was located. She worked as a cook, first for the U.S. Army and then for other people. Aunt Sally was also the first woman to have a mining claim. Later she would help nurse many children through smallpox, a deadly sickness.

Life in the Early Years

Shopkeepers opened stores along Main Street. They knew that the miners would need **supplies**, like food, clothing, and tools. Soon, teachers, lawyers, doctors, and cooks began to move to Deadwood with their families.

The families needed homes. Builders put up houses in place of the miners' tents and shacks. They also built hotels for visitors. Deadwood began to look more like a town than a mining camp.

IT'S A FACT

Around 1820, a new wave of immigrants began to arrive from countries in northern and western Europe. Members of the following groups found their way to Deadwood: English, Italians, Slovenians, Scots, Irish, French, Norwegians, Finns, Swedes, Danes, Germans, and Jewish. There were also African Americans and a large group of Chinese.

Stores replaced the tents ▶ along Main Street.

Some of the people who went to Deadwood were criminals. Deadwood was wild and lawless. The town had no sheriff, no judge, and no jail. Then something happened that really changed Deadwood.

Wild Bill Hickok came to town. Hickok was famous on the frontier as a gunfighter. He caught many outlaws. But when he came to Deadwood, Wild Bill was shot and killed while he was playing cards. People began to demand law and order.

IT'S A FACT

When Wild Bill Hickok was shot, he was holding two aces, two eights, and another card. That group of cards is now called "dead man's hand."

Gold Mining and Deadwood Change

Mining in Deadwood was changing, too. The first miners in Deadwood were **prospectors** (PRAH-spek-ters). They worked alone, panning for gold in streams. First they collected dirt and water in a pan. Then they shook the pan. If they were lucky, they would see bits of gold dust in the water. But panning was hard work, and it was getting harder to find gold that way. Many prospectors gave up and left.

◀ Most miners earned only a few dollars a day panning for gold. Few got rich.

Math Matters

Some lucky prospectors found gold dust. But how much was it worth? The price of gold went up and down. In 1877, the store owners in Deadwood decided to set a fair price for a certain weight of gold. Then prospectors would know what they could spend on things. All they had to do was have their gold weighed. That would tell them what it was worth.

There was still gold, but it was under the ground. Anyone looking for gold had to mine, or dig, for it. Gold mines had rich owners because it took money to build the mines and hire workers.

A man who worked in a mine was a different kind of miner. He didn't work by himself. He worked with other men. They helped each other. Deadwood was no longer just a mining camp. It became a mining community.

PRIMARY SOURCE

Mine owners sold shares, or parts, of their mines. People who owned shares got a piece of paper called a gold certificate.

An Immigrant Community

Many parts of the country were in the middle of a **depression** (dih-PREH-shun) in the 1870s. A depression is a time when there aren't many jobs. Many people are forced to leave their homes to look for work somewhere else. When people heard there was gold in Deadwood, they started to move to the town.

The chances of striking it rich in Deadwood were not as good as once before, but there were jobs. So people left depressed cities and towns to work in the mines around Deadwood.

▼ Deadwood, 1876

IT'S A FACT

By 1901, the Homestake Mine had produced $100 million in gold. By the time it closed in 2001, 100 years later, the digging had reached more than 8,000 feet (2,438.4 meters) below the town of Lead.

Some of the newcomers opened businesses. Sol Star originally came from Europe. Seth Bullock came from Canada. Together they opened a hardware store.

But the men did more than sell goods. Sol Star became mayor of Deadwood. He helped pass laws. Seth Bullock became the first sheriff. The two men led the way in changing Deadwood from a lawless mining camp to a more peaceful frontier town.

▼ The hardware store opened for business in 1876. It also held the town's first real post office.

They Made a Difference

People of different religions lived in Deadwood. But there was no synagogue (SIH-nuh-gahg). A synagogue is where Jewish people worship. Sol Star belonged to a group called the Masonic (muh-SAH-nik) Lodge. The Lodge had its own building. Sol Star arranged it so that Jewish miners and workers could use the Lodge building on their holy days.

There were many Chinese people in Deadwood. Some had come to America to help build the railroads. But in 1869, the major railroad lines across America were finished. The workers needed new jobs. When they heard about the mines in Deadwood, many of the Chinese immigrants went there.

Some Chinese people went into business. They opened grocery stores and restaurants. Food in the restaurants was cheap, so just about everyone could afford to eat in them.

▲ This old picture shows some of the stores the Chinese community opened.

Other Chinese people opened laundries. They washed and ironed clothes. Many miners didn't have places to wash their things. Some people said that the laundries washed gold dust out of the miners' clothes.

By 1880, the Chinese had formed a community called Chinatown. There were stores there that sold goods from China. Chinatown had its own policemen. The community even had its own fire truck.

▼ The Chinese had their own police and firemen in Chinatown.

Eyewitness Account

Estelline Bennett wrote a book about growing up in Deadwood. In the book, she wrote about the many different communities in town: *"We had come so far in the nineteenth century as to believe that Deadwood Gulch was wide enough for as many races as could find it."*

In 1890, the railroad came to Deadwood. People traveled by train to visit the mines and see the sights. There were grand hotels for the visitors to stay in.

Several famous people came to Deadwood, too. Calamity Jane and Buffalo Bill Cody were two of them. They performed in Wild West shows. Nat Love, an African American cowboy, also performed in Deadwood.

Calamity Jane's real name was ▶ Martha Canary. According to one story, she warned people that if they upset her, it would be a calamity, a very bad thing, for them.

PRIMARY SOURCE

Buffalo Bill went to Deadwood by railroad. Someone heard him say, "A town is young just as long as it stays off the railroad." But he also said that a town "either grows up or it dies." Deadwood had grown up.

Nat Love earned the ▶ nickname "Deadwood Dick" when he won a contest for cowboys in Deadwood.

In the 1900s, Deadwood began to fade. The nearby gold mines closed. Some men left Deadwood to find work in the gold mines of Nevada and Alaska. Some families bought land in other states and started farms. Many people in the Chinese community returned to China.

There was still work around Deadwood mining other minerals. There were also jobs lumbering, or cutting and preparing trees for sale. But the town's population continued to fall. Fewer people meant less business for the town's shops and restaurants.

◀ Every prospector dreamed of finding a solid gold nugget like this one.

Historical Perspective

Today it costs too much to dig for gold the old way. Now gold miners use all sorts of machines. But first they have to find enough ore. Ore is a rock or mineral with gold in it. It might take 6,000 pounds (2,721 kilograms) of ore to get one ounce (28 grams) of gold.

A Historical Community

A lot of people in Deadwood owned land, houses, stores, and hotels there. They didn't want to leave their property behind. And what about the people who worked for them? They would have to leave, too. If everyone left, Deadwood would become another ghost town.

There are many ghost towns in the West, and townspeople didn't want Deadwood to become like them. They wanted the town to be as it once was. They wanted Deadwood to be lively and full of people again.

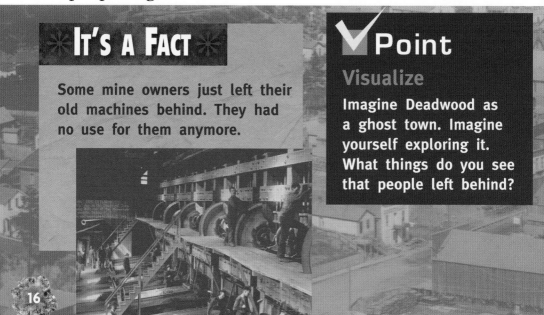

☀ IT'S A FACT ☀

Some mine owners just left their old machines behind. They had no use for them anymore.

✔Point

Visualize

Imagine Deadwood as a ghost town. Imagine yourself exploring it. What things do you see that people left behind?

Finally, in 1987, officials set up a group to think of ways to help the town. It was called the Historic **Preservation** (preh-zer-VAY-shun) Commission. Preservation means keeping something from getting damaged or falling apart. In this case, the officials decided that the buildings in Deadwood should be preserved and restored, or fixed up to look the way they did in the past.

The leaders of the group reminded people of the importance of Deadwood's history. In 1961, Deadwood had been named a National Historic Landmark. That meant that all of Deadwood should be preserved because it was special.

▼ Deadwood was a busy town in 1880. People wanted to keep it that way.

PRIMARY SOURCE

Just how famous is Deadwood around the world? In the 1960s, the Beatles, a popular English singing group, recorded the song "Rocky Raccoon." The song begins, "Now, somewhere in the black mountain hills of Dakota/There lived a young boy named Rocky Raccoon." It goes on to tell of Rocky's adventures in the wild, lawless town of Deadwood.

The members of the commission knew that many **tourists** visited South Dakota every year. Tourists are people who travel for fun. Many tourists like to go to places with interesting histories.

Since people still told stories about Deadwood's colorful past, the commission thought that tourists might like to visit the town to learn about its history.

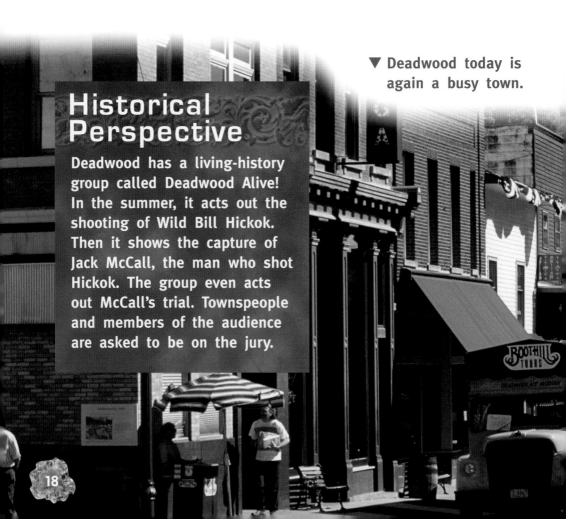

▼ Deadwood today is again a busy town.

Historical Perspective

Deadwood has a living-history group called Deadwood Alive! In the summer, it acts out the shooting of Wild Bill Hickok. Then it shows the capture of Jack McCall, the man who shot Hickok. The group even acts out McCall's trial. Townspeople and members of the audience are asked to be on the jury.

Main Street really hadn't changed that much from the old days. Some of the buildings just needed to be restored in the right way.

The officials also planned events that would remind people of old-time Deadwood. They wanted to make visitors feel as though they were stepping back in time.

▼ Bullock's is still in Deadwood today as a hotel.

There was already a museum in town. It was the idea of a wealthy man named W.E. Adams. He made his money by selling supplies to miners.

In 1930, he added a museum to his house. He wanted to preserve some of the objects that were part of the history of the Black Hills. Today it is called the Adams Museum & House.

Careers

Museum Curator

Curators (KYER-ay-terz) are the people who care for the things in museum exhibits. They know a lot about the history of each piece. Curators can explain to museum visitors how the things were once used. Some museums collect things from a certain time in history. A museum exhibit in Deadwood might include mining tools that a prospector used long ago.

▼ This is how the Adams Museum & House looks today.

The commission's plan worked. Tourists did travel to Deadwood. They still do. They visit the museum. They go inside the restored buildings. They can even tour a real gold mine. They get a feeling for what Deadwood was like in the past.

Deadwood's streets are crowded with people now. They arrive from all over. And many want to visit again.

History has given Deadwood another chance. Now it is once again a frontier community.

IT'S A FACT

Many tourists visit the Mount Moriah (muh-RY-uh) Cemetery in Deadwood. They look for the markers of famous people, like Calamity Jane and Wild Bill Hickok. They are buried near each other. They also visit the different sections of the cemetery. The Jewish community and the Chinese community had their own sections.

◀ Many people visit the grave of Wild Bill Hickok.

21

Conclusion

Deadwood began as a gold-mining camp. Then it became a town. There were stores and other businesses. There was a government. People came from many places to live and work in Deadwood.

Then the mines closed. The town seemed on the way to becoming a ghost town. But the town's leaders tried something new. They fixed up the old buildings. They used them to tell people about the town's history, and the old Deadwood came to life. Today, Deadwood is a busy historic community.

✔ Point

Think About It

What people helped Deadwood in the past? What can people do to keep Deadwood alive today?

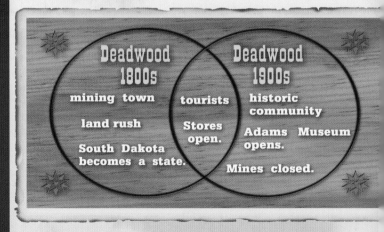

Deadwood 1800s
- mining town
- land rush
- South Dakota becomes a state.

tourists
Stores open.

Deadwood 1900s
- historic community
- Adams Museum opens.
- Mines closed.

Glossary

depression (dih-PREH-shun) a time when business is slow and people are out of work (page 10)

frontier (frun-TEER) the far edge of a country where people are just beginning to settle (page 3)

gold rush (GOLD RUSH) when people hurry to a place to look for gold that has been discovered there (page 3)

gulch (GULCH) a narrow valley with steep, rocky sides (page 2)

homestead (HOME-sted) to get government land on which to farm (page 4)

population (pah-pyuh-LAY-shun) the people living in a place (page 5)

preservation (preh-zer-VAY-shun) fixing something old while keeping it true to the past (page 17)

prospector (PRAH-spek-ter) a person who looks for a valuable natural resource (page 8)

supplies (suh-PLIZE) food, clothing, and tools (page 6)

territory (TAIR-ih-tor-ee) land that is under the control of a distant government (page 3)

tourist (TOR-ist) a person who travels for pleasure (page 18)

Index